Discovering My World

From Chick to Robin

by Melvin and Gilda Berger

W9-BNC-659

SCHOLASTIC INC.

New York   Toronto   London   Auckland
Sydney   Mexico City   New Delhi   Hong Kong

ISBN 978-0-545-24455-8

12 11 10 9 8 7 6 5 4 3 2   11 12 13 14 15 16/0

Printed in the U.S.A.   40
First printing, April 2011

Photo Credits:

Cover: © NightAndDayImages/iStockphoto; Back cover: © Lightscapes Inc./Photolibrary; Title page: © Darlyne A. Murawski/Getty Images; Page 3: © Graham De'ath/Shutterstock; Page 4: © William Leaman/Alamy; Page 5: © Stone Nature Photography/Alamy; Page 6: © Vishnevskiy Vasily/Shutterstock; Page 7: © National Geographic Image Collection/ Alamy; Page 8: © peterspiro/iStockphoto; Page 9: © Kenneth C. Zirkel/iStockphoto; Page 10: © Ron Willocks/Animals Animals; Page 11: © Jupiterimages/Getty Images/Thinkstock; Page 12: © Russell Burden/Photolibrary; Page 13: © Helmut Heintges/Photolibrary; Page 14: © Rolf Nussbaumer/Photolibrary; Page 15: © Rolf Nussbaumer Photography/ Alamy; Page 16: © Thinkstock

Robins sing in the spring.

How do robins carry the grass?

Robins gather dry grass.

They build a nest.

What color
are the
eggs?

The mother lays three to five eggs.

She sits on the eggs.

The eggs hatch.

How many chicks do you see?

The chicks are hungry.

The father helps feed the chicks.

Where is the nest?

He guards the nest.

Do you see their feathers?

The young robins learn to fly.

Soon they fly away.

Robins feed on fruit and berries.

Is the worm in the ground?

This robin found a juicy worm to eat!

Ask Yourself

1. When do robins sing?

2. What do robins use to build a nest?

3. How many eggs do robins lay?

4. Who helps feed the chicks?

5. What do robins eat?

You can find the answers in this book.